Mud Puddle Books
NEW YORK

Contents

Making
Sock Puppets
Tips & Techniques for Fabulous Fun!
Text and Puppets Created by
Diana Schoenbrun
Photographed by F. William Lagaret
Mud Puddle Books
Painting on Glass Stones
Tips & Techniques for Fabulous Fun!
Illustrated by Raffaella Dowling
Text by Jessica Dowling
Photography by F. William Lagaret
Mud Puddle Books
Creating with Cool Clay
By Ruby Shumaker
Mud Puddle Books
Painting on Rocks
Tips & Techniques for Fabulous Fun
Illustrated by Raffaella, Jessica, and Devin Dowling
Photography by F. William Lagaret
Text by Jessica Dowling
Mud Puddle Books
Making Friendship Bracelets
By Kaylee Conner
Mud Puddle Books

Making Sock Puppets

Tips & Techniques for Fabulous Fun!

Text and Puppets Created by

Diana Schoenbrun

Photographed by F. William Lagaret

Mud Puddle Books
NEW YORK

Making Sock Puppets: Tips & Techniques for Fabulous Fun
Text and puppets created by Diana Schoenbrun.
Photography by F. William Lagaret.

Mud Puddle Books, Inc.
54 W. 21st Street
Suite 601
New York, NY 10010
info@mudpuddlebooks.com

ISBN: 978-1-60311-056-3

Designed by Michelle Gengaro

Printed and bound in China

Sock Puppet Creations

Ever have dreams of being a puppeteer? Sock puppets are a great way to start. Everyone can enjoy them and the fun is infectious. Sock puppets are so easy to make because they are made from materials that are found around the house. Just give free reign to your imagination and you'll soon be making animals, people, monsters and other creatures.

Creating a sock puppet is just the start of the fun. You'll find that sock puppets can be used in a variety of mirthful ways.

For example, making up stories is particularly exciting when you have 3-dimensional characters that can play the roles. Both children and adults can use their puppets for storytelling. Try reading from a book or play, and act out the scenes with the puppets. Make a whole cast of different sock puppet characters and then invite your friends and family to put on a puppet show.

Or throw a sock puppet party and have everyone bring a sock and extra materials to share. Write down different characters on separate pieces of paper. Put the paper in a hat and have everyone pick a character to create.

Sock puppets can be used to make learning more fun. Use sock puppets to help learn the alphabet or counting. Why not use a puppet to practice singing a song? Communicating new ideas with the puppets is easy because puppetry is exciting and holds everyone's attention.

Making sock puppets allows you to be creative and nothing makes a better gift than something you create. Give a friend a sock puppet that looks like their favorite pet or make one that looks just like them!

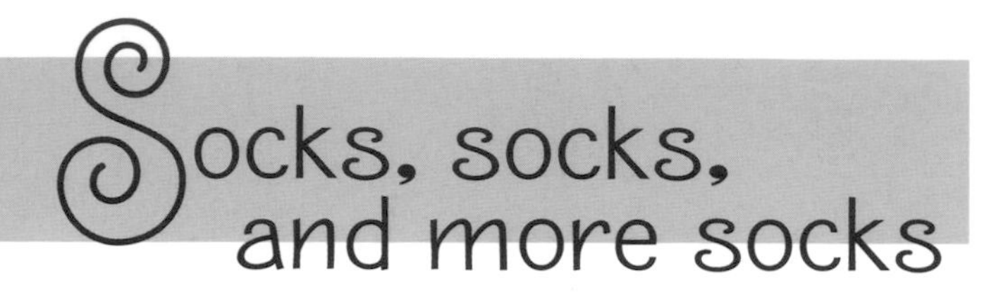

Socks, socks, and more socks

There are so many types of socks to choose from when designing a sock puppet. Best of all, you can use socks with holes or socks that no longer fit. Recycling in this way is certainly better than throwing away. Collect unwanted socks from friends and family. Use a sock that has lost its match. Turn a sock inside out if you want a fuzzy texture. Most importantly, always remember to wash your socks before making your puppet. Look in your sock drawer and you may find that you already have a treasure trove of unwanted socks, all of which would be great for making sock puppets.

Look for socks such as these:

- **stretchy socks**
- **cotton crew socks**
- **tube socks**
- **athletic gym socks**
- **toe socks**
- **novelty socks**
- **knee high socks**
- **trouser socks**
- **ankle socks**
- **wool socks**
- **striped socks**
- **patterned socks**
- **slouchy socks**
- **pom pom socks**

getting started

Here are some of things you might use to make spectacular sock puppets. Most of these materials can be found at home or at art and craft stores.

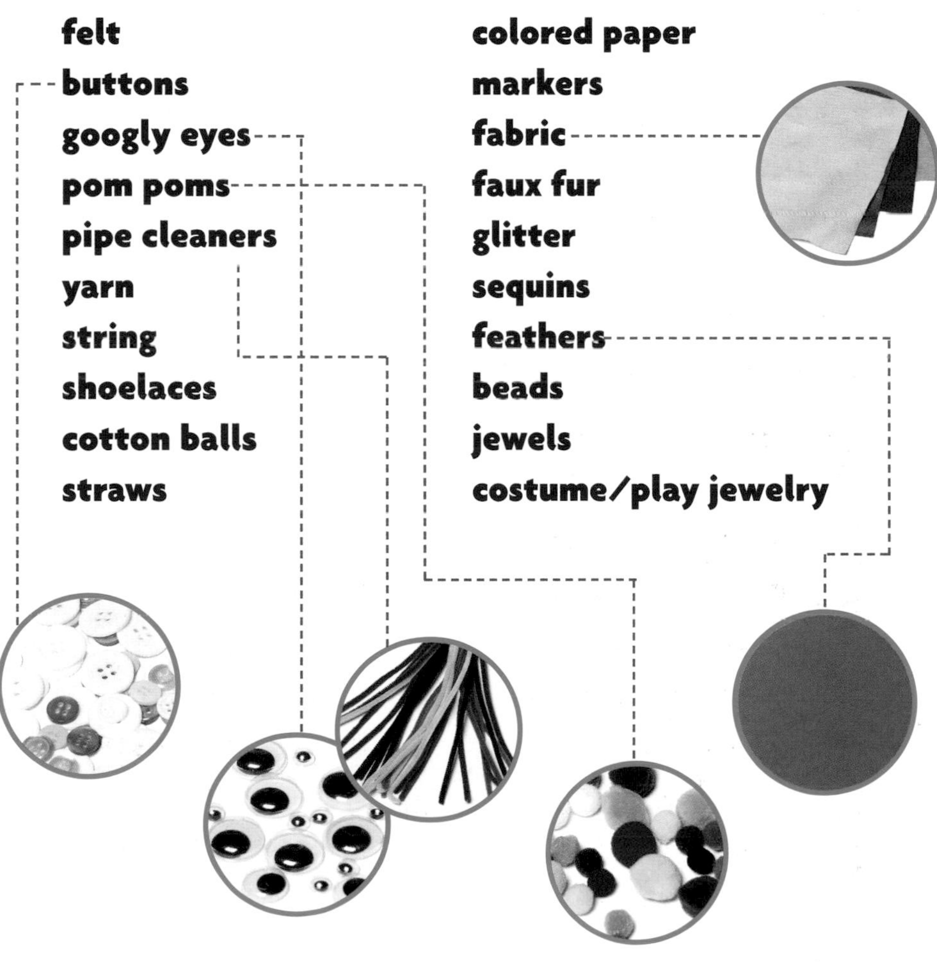

felt
buttons
googly eyes
pom poms
pipe cleaners
yarn
string
shoelaces
cotton balls
straws
colored paper
markers
fabric
faux fur
glitter
sequins
feathers
beads
jewels
costume/play jewelry

Other helpful tools

Craft glue is good for attaching materials to your sock. It makes a stronger bond than a basic school glue or glue stick.

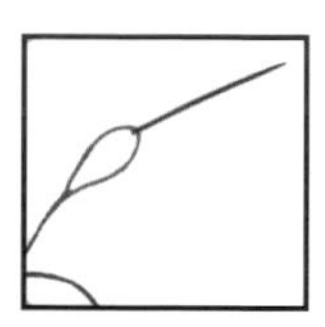

Needle and thread may be used as well for attaching pieces. Always ask an adult for help when sewing.

Scissors for cutting. Be careful using scissors and have an adult help.

Making your sock puppet

Eyes can be made using buttons, felt, googly eyes, and pom poms. You can also draw eyes using a fabric marker.

Noses can be made from buttons, pom poms, and felt. The nose can be as detailed as you like.

Make nostrils by pinching the sock together in the center

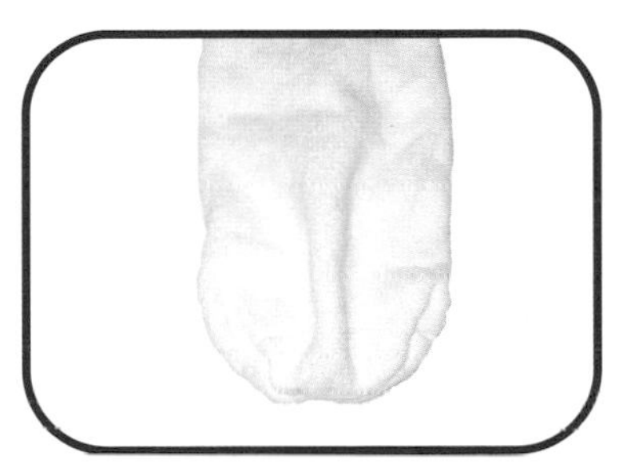

and add a few stitches to secure.

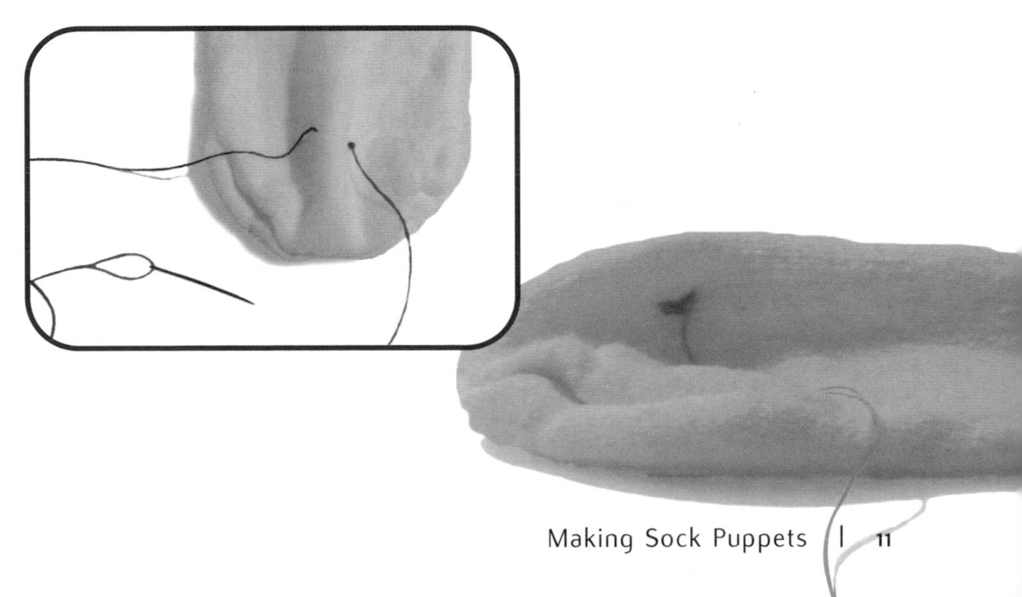

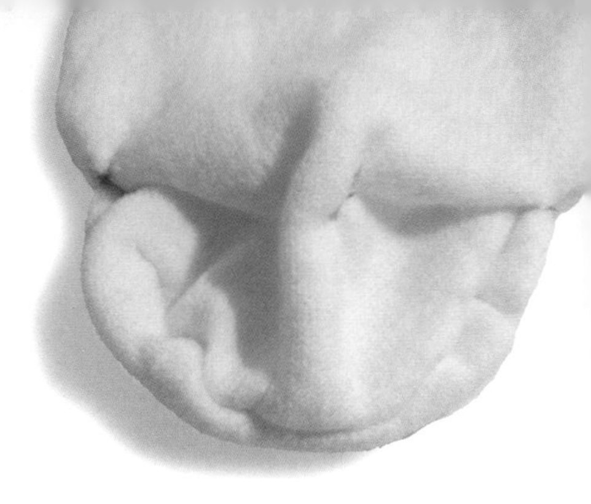

Next pinch the sock fabric forward on each side to create two nostrils. Sew a few stitches on the left and right side to secure.

Then cut a piece of felt shaped like the letter 'm'.

Glue or sew each side underneath the centerpiece.

Now cover the nostrils with the felt snout.

Use glue or sew to secure.

Mouths can be formed a few ways.

The easiest way to create a mouth would be to use the natural fold of the sock.

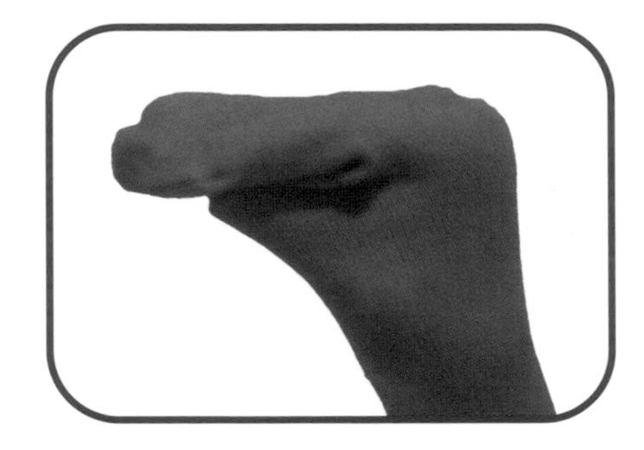

It's easy to add detail to the mouth by gluing or sewing a felt tongue in the sock fold.

For an even more detailed mouth, glue or sew a dark colored fabric oval on the sock and place a felt tongue in the center of the oval. Finally, felt teeth can be added around the mouth.

Ears can be made from felt, fabric, and paper.

Cut different shapes for ears depending on your character. Attach ears with craft glue or stitch them onto the sock with a needle and thread.

Hair can be made from yarn, string, or ribbon.

For yarn hair cut a 5 to 7 inch (12.7 to 17.8 cm) strand. Loop the yarn and knot at one end.

Cut additional strands and knot each in the center around the original strand.

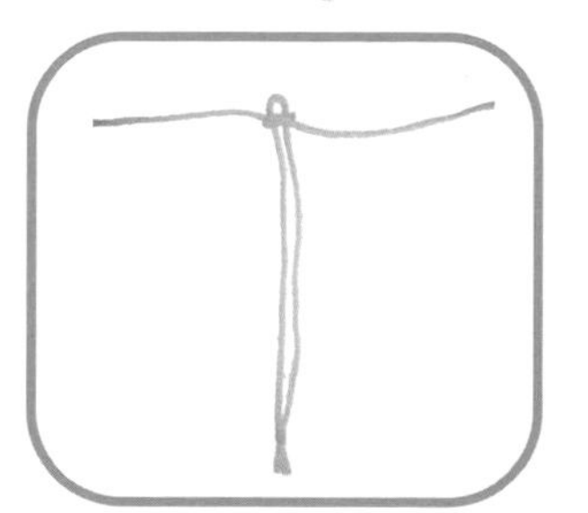

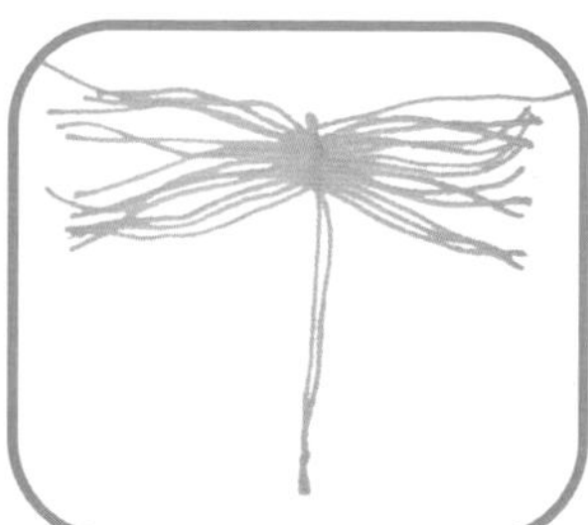

You're creating a sock toupee!

Use glue to attach
to the sock.

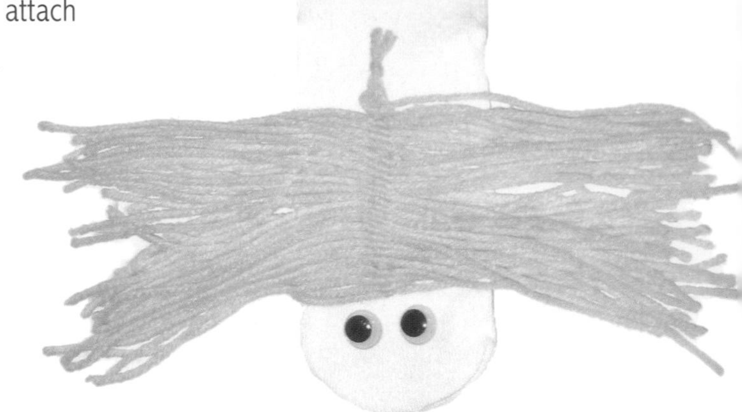

Felt can also be cut to create a mane of hair. Faux fur is fun to use too.

Tails can be made many different ways. Pom poms and cotton balls are perfect for shorter tails. Long tails can be made from ribbon, yarn, string, shoelaces, and felt.

You can cut a single strand of felt for a simple tail.

If you'd like a bushy look, cut the end of the felt.

Use a shoelace for a longer tail and, if you'd like, unravel the end of the shoelace for a bushy effect.

A more complicated tail can be made with a pipe cleaner and felt. Bend the pipe cleaner in half and twist. Leave a small loop at one end.

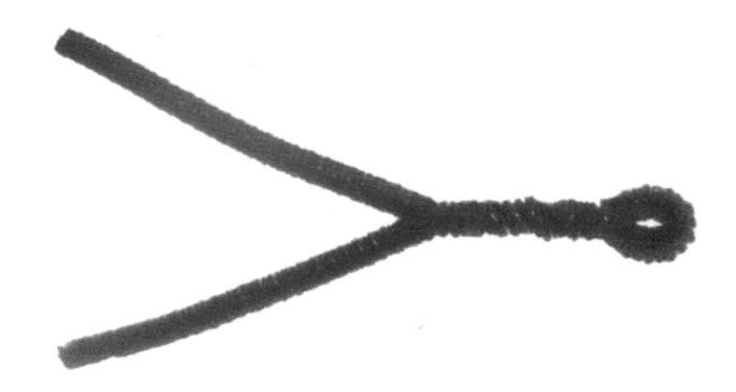

Cut the end of a felt strand to fray and wrap it around the pipe cleaner.

Then secure the felt
with craft glue or sew
a few stitches to hold.

Sew through the
pipe cleaner loop and
attach the tail to the sock.

Whiskers are easily made with pipe cleaners.

Three small pipe cleaners can be used.

Twist two pieces at the center twice to form an X.

Then take the third pipe cleaner and twist around the center of the first two pipe cleaners.

Sew the whiskers to the sock at the center of the pipe cleaners before adding a nose.

Antenna can also be made with pipe cleaners.

The easiest way is to fold
a pipe cleaner in half
and bend any way you wish.

To make the antenna sturdier and flexible,
twist two pipe cleaners together.

Bend the pipe cleaners in half at the center
and flatten slightly.

Sewing pom poms on the ends
makes an interesting effect.

Finally attach the antennae to the sock by adding a few stitches where the pipe cleaner is bent.

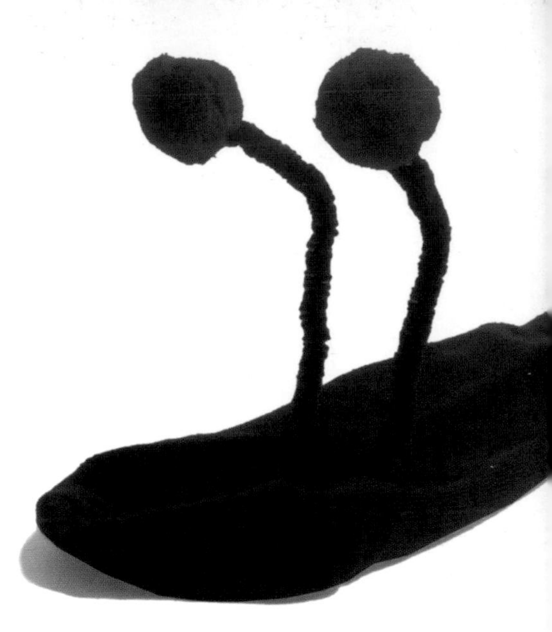

Accessories can make your puppet more unique. Add glitter and gems to make your sock puppets sparkle. Jewelry and beads are good materials to dress them up.

flamingo

pig

flower

bee

rabbit

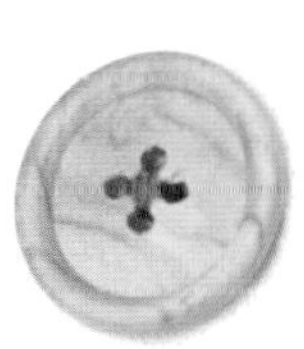

cat

princess

lion

Painting on Glass Stones

Tips & Techniques for Fabulous Fun!

Illustrated by Raffaella Dowling

Text by Jessica Dowling

Photography by F. William Lagaret

Mud Puddle Books
NEW YORK

Painting on Glass Stones
Illustrated by Raffaella Dowling
Text by Jessica Dowling
Photography by F. William Lagaret

Mud Puddle Books, Inc.
54 W. 21st Street
Suite 601
New York, NY 10010
info@mudpuddlebooks.com

ISBN: 1-59412-152-4

Designed by Tasha Sakhrani

Printed and bound in China

Painting on glass stones is a fun and easy way to make your own miniature treasures!

All you need to get started is a glass stone, some paint, a brush and your own imagination. Remember, the technique used to paint on the glass is very different from the technique you would normally use to paint on a surface…in fact, it is the exact opposite!

The glass stone has two sides: one rounded, and one flat. You paint the flat side, wait for it to dry, and then view your design from the rounded side. This magnifies the design you've made and gives it a unique look. Here's the catch: you have to paint the foreground first and the background last.

For instance, if you were painting a glass stone to look like a smiley face, you would first paint the mouth and the eyes. After waiting for this to dry completely, you would then paint the background color of the face. When this dries, you flip it around to reveal your reverse-painted work of art! Once you get used to it, it is a very simple technique.

There is no need to paint complicated subjects. Because of the way the stone magnifies and intensifies your design, even a tern of stripes or dots painted on the stone will look great! Glass stones are the perfect medium to try abstract art.

Keep in mind everything that you paint on the back of the glass stone will appear in reverse when you flip it over! If you want to paint a letter, make sure you paint it backwards on the flat side of the rock.

If you make a mistake with a glass stone, don't worry! Drop the painted stone in a cup of warm water for a few minutes. This will loosen the paint. Then, using a sponge, scrub your design off the glass stone. Make sure you use a sponge that isn't being used to clean dishes or other food

utensils. Dry your stone with paper towels and start over! When you have assembled a collection of painted glass stones, there are many things you can do with them. They make great gifts for parents, teachers, or anyone else! By cutting a piece of self-adhesive magnetic backing (available at craft stores) to fit the back of a painted stone, you can make a set of unique, colorful magnets. A painted glass stone hot-glued to a flat thumbtack makes an original pushpin for a bulletin board. Even something as simple as arranging your stones on a desk or table will look great!

They make great gifts!

Materials

- **Acrylic Paint -** A good starter set would contain white, black, red, blue and yellow paint. You can mix these basic paints to create colors like purple, pink, and green. Fine arts acrylics cost a little more than craft acrylics but provide a much thicker coat of paint. This can lessen the amount of coats you have to apply when painting on a clear surface.
- **Very fine acrylic brushes -** Sizes 0 and 1 work well because the surface you are painting is so small.
- **Toothpicks -** When painting glass stones, these can work just as well as brushes!
- **A cup of water** to clean brushes.
- **Paper towels** for surface cleanup.
- **Newspaper** to lay on top of your work area to protect surfaces.

HOLIDAY

HEARTS

FLOWERS

TIP

Always remember- when painting glass stones, you paint "in reverse"! This means the foreground goes on first, and the background last!

ANIMALS

BUGS

OCEAN

TIP

Make sure to take a break from painting every so often to give your hands and eyes a rest.

SPORTS

ALPHABET

D
E
F
K
L
M
Q
R
S
W
Y
T
X
Z

More Great Tips!

Try to think of creative backgrounds for your subject matter. Don't always use white! Try bright colors, stripes, or even polka dots as a backdrop for your creations.

If you decide you don't like a finished glass stone, soak it for a while in a glass of hot water, and rub the paint off with a dry paper towel.

Try not to water down the paint too much. The thicker the paint, the better it will adhere to the glass.

Change the water you use to clean your brushes often, to prevent muddy colors.

Don't leave brushes in your cup of water! This can cause the bristles and handle of your brush to get ruined. After washing your brushes, lay them on some paper towels to dry until you need them again. Well cared for brushes can last years!

After your designs are completely dry, give the underside of the glass stone a coat of clear acrylic to prevent your design from rubbing off.

Good lighting conditions are key! Make sure you are working in bright light. This will allow you to see colors clearly, and keep your eyes from working too hard.

Toothpicks are one of the most useful tools for painting glass stones. Dipping one in a small amount of paint allows you to create fine details and designs.

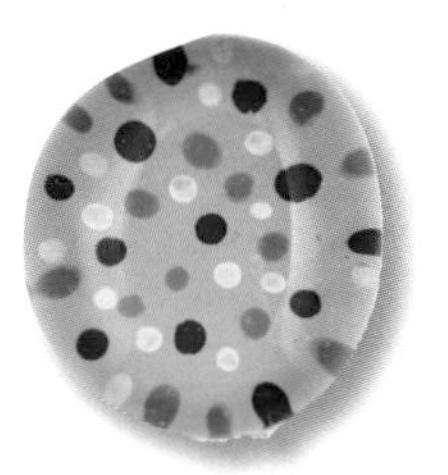

Sketch Area

Use this area to sketch some of your own ideas for painting stones!

Creating with Cool Clay

By Ruby Shumaker

Mud Puddle Books
NEW YORK

Mud Puddle Books, Inc.
54 W. 21st Street Suite 601
New York, NY 10010
info@mudpuddlebooks.com

ISBN: 978-1-60311-106-5

Hand model: Madison Hogge

Printed in China

Introduction

Kinds of Clay

There are many different kinds of clay that can be used for modeling. Each has advantages and disadvantages, depending on what it is that you want to make from the clay that you are using.

Modeling Clay:

- Modeling clay is nontoxic and safe for all ages to use.
- It will not harden, even if left unprotected. This means it can be used over and over again.
- This clay cannot be used for permanent creations, because it will remain soft. For example, you cannot make jewelry that you want to wear from modeling clay.
- It is best to make small objects from modeling clay, because it is very heavy and will not hold its shape for larger items.

- Modeling clay can usually be found in the kid's craft section of your local craft or hobby store.

  NOTE: Some of the modeling clay found in the kid's craft section is Play Dough®. It is made from a softer compound and is more difficult to mold into smaller shapes than modeling clay. It is, however, easier for younger children to use.

Clay Dough:

- Made at home from cooking ingredients, clay dough is nontoxic and safe for all ages to use.
- Although softer than modeling clay, clay dough can also be used over and over again.
- Clay dough can be hardened in the oven like polymer clay.
- Store in an airtight container in the refrigerator to prevent drying and cracking.

Polymer Clay:

- Polymer clay is nontoxic and safe for all ages to use.
- Polymer clay should be soft when purchased. If you purchase clay that is too hard to knead, there are clay softeners available at your local craft store.

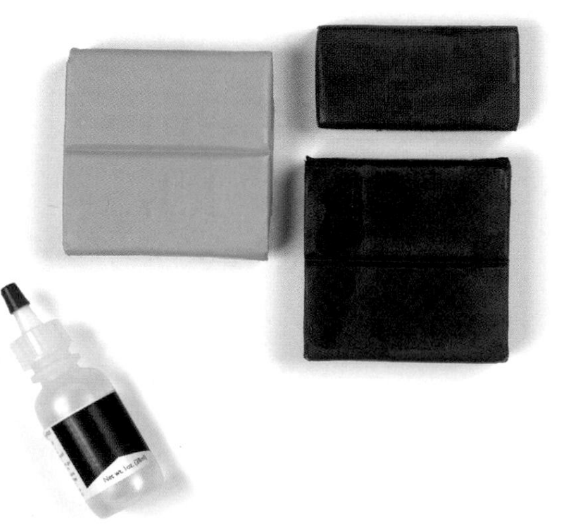

- This clay does not dry out while you are working with it, so you don't need to hurry to make a project from it.
- Bake polymer clay in the oven to create permanent projects. It will not shrink or change size but some of the clays will change color after being baked.

color before baked color after baked

- Polymer clay should not be used to make food containers or to hold items that burn, such as candles or incense.

Working with Clays

Modeling Clay:

- Wash your hands before working with modeling clay, and between working with different colors.
- Work on a flat, clean, dry surface that is covered with a plastic sheet or disposable vinyl tablecloth.
- Knead clay before molding to soften.
- When creating a project, try working with the lighter colors first, then moving on to darker colors. This will help prevent colors from smearing onto other clays.
- If the clay sticks to your modeling tools, carefully remove as much clay as you can with a toothpick or butter knife. Clean utensils with a small scrub brush or toothbrush (one used only for clay) and warm, soapy water.

- Store clay in airtight containers or plastic bags that have all the air squished out.

Clay Dough:

- All of the instructions under Modeling Clay apply to clay dough.
- Most clay dough will dry out during use, so additional water may be needed to prevent cracking.
- Some types of clay dough can be eaten! These types of clay are used for decorating cookies, cakes, and cupcakes. Be sure to wash your hands when working with different colors to prevent mixing. Store edible clay dough in the refrigerator and clean up with warm, soapy water.

Polymer Clays:

- All of the instructions under Modeling Clay apply to polymer clays.
- To work with polymer clay, pinch, squeeze, squish, and knead as much clay as you need until it is soft enough to roll into a snake. Fold the snake over on itself a few times, roll into a snake again, and fold. Try not to get any air bubbles into the clay. Fold and roll until the ends of the clay stretch instead of break when you pull the ends.

- Polymer clay will stay soft until you bake it in the oven. Always follow the manufacturer's instructions for baking and always ask a grown-up to help you use the oven. NEVER put polymer clay in the microwave.
- You can make additions to your already-baked polymer creations by adding fresh, unbaked details and putting them back into the oven. If pieces do not stick while in the oven, use white glue to adhere them together.

General Tips:

- If tools are sticking to your clay, brush a little cornstarch on the clay.
- If polymer clay is sticking to your hands, wipe your hands with a small amount of baby oil.
- To remove polymer clay from your hands, use hand lotion to break down the clay. Wipe off with a paper towel, then wash with warm, soapy water.

Tools and Other Cool Stuff

You can use almost anything you want to when working with clay! Once you have used a tool for clay, it should not be used for anything else. Be sure to ask a grown-up which tools are okay for you to use. Here are some ideas:

Plastic Rolling Pin: A small rolling pin is best when trying to flatten clay evenly. Use a plastic rolling pin, not a wooden one, because the wooden one will leave marks on the clay and the clay will absorb into the wood.

A rolling pin found in the cake decorating section of your local craft or hobby store is usually a good one to use with clay. It is used for fondant* and has elastic on each end to act as a thickness guide. If your rolling pin does not have elastics, use two craft sticks on each side of the clay you are rolling to help keep the dough the same thickness.

Cutting Tools: Table knives and forks or plastic knives and forks are good for cutting and making patterns in your clay. Do not use sharp knives. You can use household items such as scissors or an egg slicer to cut your clay, or special craft

*A thick sugar and water mixture used both in the making of candy and the icing and decorating of cakes. Can be flavored and colored.

knives used with clay or rolling cutters used in fondant frosting designs.

Pattern Makers: Toothpicks and straws can be used to punch holes, or make small dots or patterns in your clay. You can also use items such as pencils, skewers, forks, paintbrushes, or whatever you can find in the drawer. Modeling tool kits made especially to work with clay or items used with fondant frosting can be purchased in your local craft store.

NOTE: Whenever using scissors, knives, or cutters ask for a grown-up's help.

Cookie Cutters or Clay Cutters: Cookie cutters come in all shapes and sizes and are an easy way to make shapes in your clay. Clay cutters are also available in the clay section of your craft and hobby store. A clay press or extruder also has many of the same shapes as a cookie cutter or clay cutter.

Tracing Objects: Stencils and household items can be used to trace shapes onto clay.

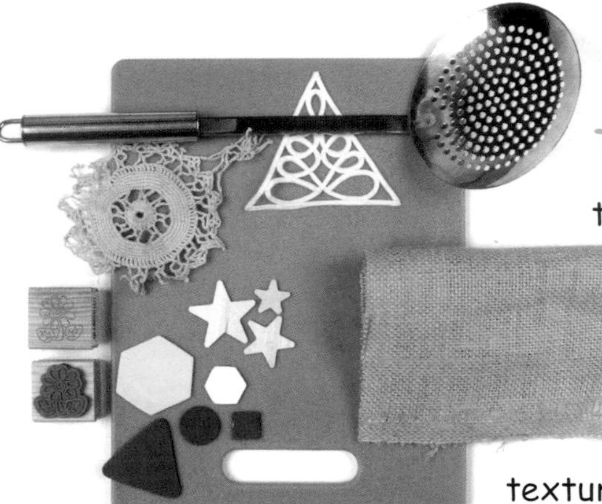

Texturing Tools: Texturing tools are whatever you want to use that will create patterns in your clay. You can use rubber stamps, textured fabric such as burlap, kitchen utensils, or wood cutouts.

Garlic Press or Clay Press: A garlic press is one of the best tools when working with clay and can be purchased in the kitchen section of most stores. A garlic press is limited to one size of clay "strings".

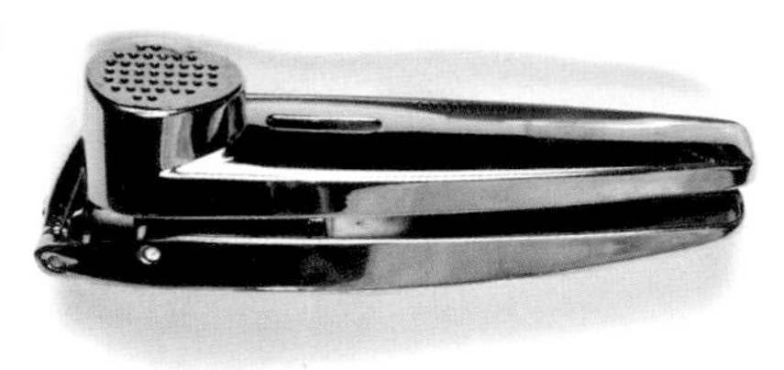

A clay press is similar to a garlic press; only it has a variety of inserts that can regulate the size and shape of the clay as it is squeezed through the press. This tool is often called an "extruder".

In the projects in this book you can use either a garlic press or an extruder, depending on which is best for your needs.

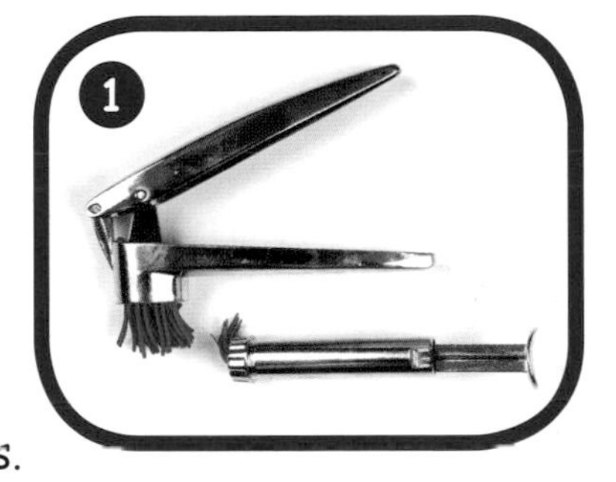

Neither, however, are easy objects to clean. When using a press in a project that requires many colors, do not wash the press between colors.

1 Squeeze as much as possible of the first color clay through the press, 2 then squeeze the second color through. When the first color is finished and just a small amount of the second color appears, trim that and 3 begin the second color for the project. Continue in this manner with as many colors as are needed for the project.

Cookie Sheet: When working with polymer clay, you will want to create your projects on a cookie sheet covered in tin foil so that you can easily put them in the oven for baking.

Embellishments: When working with clay you can use anything you want to embellish your designs. Try using feathers, buttons, rhinestones, tiny paper flags or umbrellas, rubber animals, pom-poms, or whatever else your imagination can find.

Miscellaneous Items

Small Watercolor Brush: This is used to apply a small amount of water to the clay when two pieces are joined together.

Vinyl Tablecloth or Plastic Sheet: This is used to cover your work surface. It is a good idea to have a large plastic sheet as well as squares of plastic that can be used for each individual color of clay.

Tool Box: It is a good idea to have a box for storing clay and tools. This way, you will always know where they are and no one will mistake them for cooking tools! Decorate it any way you want so that everyone knows it is your clay box!

Clay Shapes

Now that you know what kinds of clay there are and what tools to use, it is time to actually make something with your clay. You may want to practice making a few shapes before you begin a project, but remember: It's only clay! If you make a mistake, you can knead the clay again and start over. And sometimes, mistakes can make the best projects of all!

Shapes

- Most projects are made from a few basic shapes. Once you master these easy shapes, you can make anything!

- These shapes are called for throughout the book in almost every project. If you do not know how to make one of the shapes refer back to these instructions.

- You will have to practice making shapes until you can guess how much clay you will need for a project. If you create your shape and it's not big enough, get more clay, knead the two pieces together, and reshape. The same is true if the piece is too large. Remove some of the clay, knead the piece again, and reshape.

- Do not make your shapes too large or too heavy. It is better to make smaller projects from the kinds of clay that are described in this book.

Ball:

1. Squish a piece of clay together with your fingers and then gently roll it into a ball between the palms of your hand.

2. Continue rolling, using even pressure with both hands until it is perfectly smooth and round.

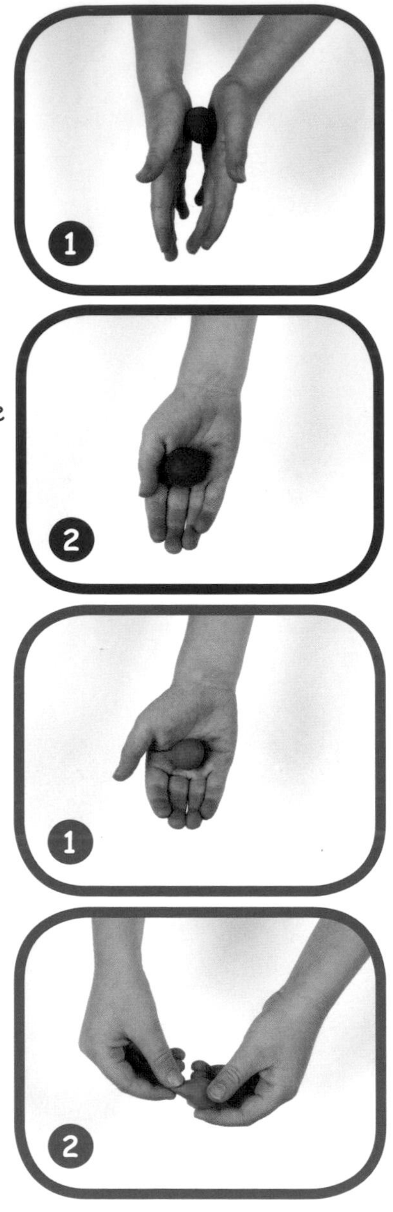

Cone:

1. Create a ball shape following the Ball instructions.

2. Take the finished ball and pinch an end into a point.

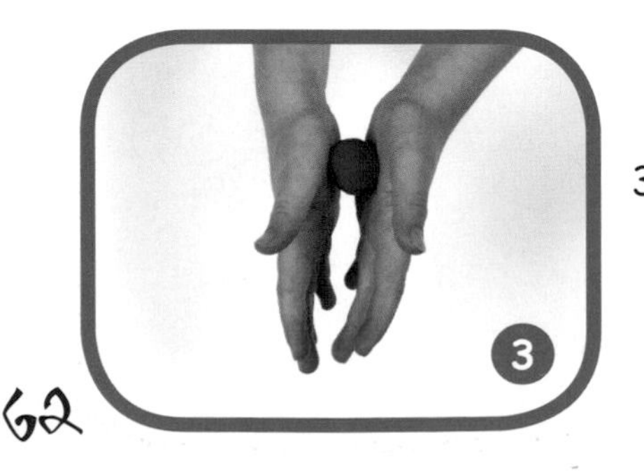

3. Roll this shape gently between your palms to keep the base round.

4. Press the rounded end of your ball onto a flat surface.

Oval:

1. Create a ball shape following the Ball instructions.

2. Now roll the ball back and forth between your hands, pressing a little more firmly than you did when rolling it into a ball.

3. Do this until the shape is longer and the ends become narrower. You now have an oval.

Sausage:

1. Create a ball shape following the Ball instructions.

2. Take the ball and roll it back and forth between the palms of your hands until it becomes longer and forms a thick sausage shape.

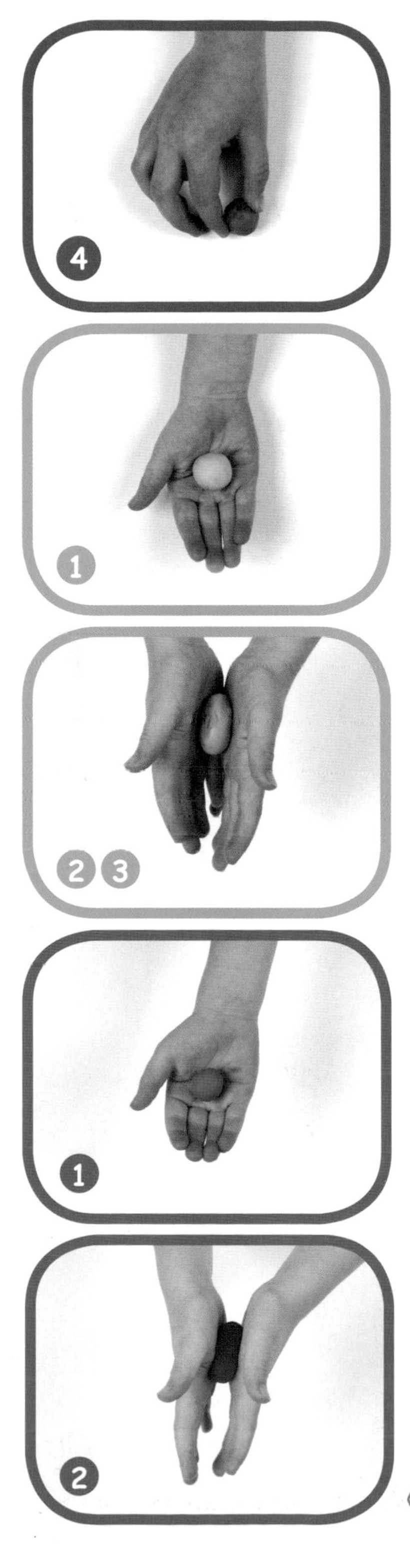

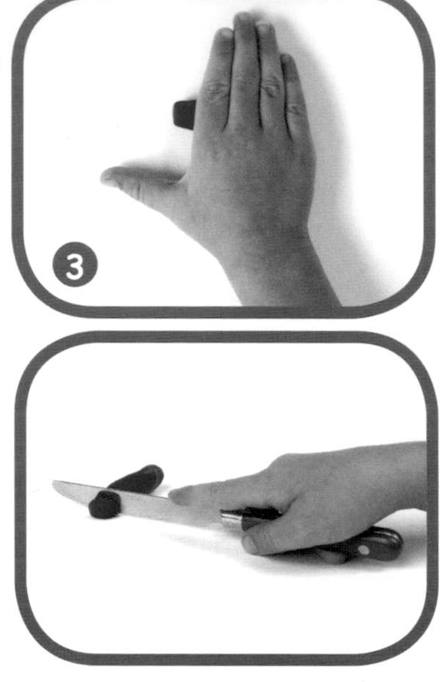

3. Next place this shape onto a tabletop and continue rolling with the palm of one hand until it is the length and the thickness that you want.

Hint: You can finish the ends by leaving them the way they are, cutting them with a knife, flattening them against the table, or pinching them off.

Rope:

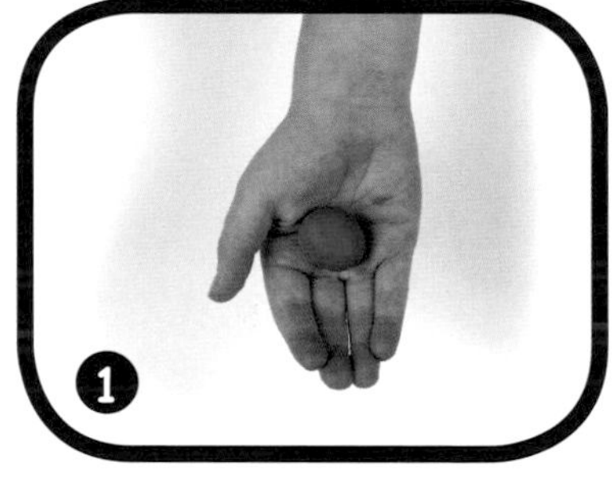

1. Create a ball shape following the Ball instructions.

2. Lay the ball on a flat surface and use your fingers and equal pressure to roll and stretch the ball out into a rope.

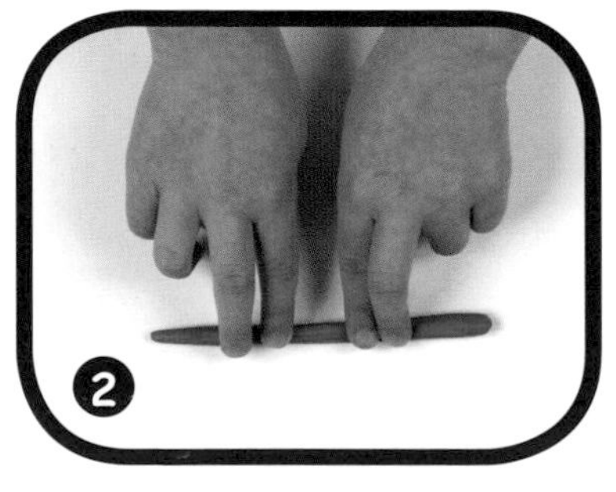

3. Continue rolling and stretching until it is the length and the thickness needed for the project. It will take a little practice to get a rope that is even in thickness from end to end.

Strips:

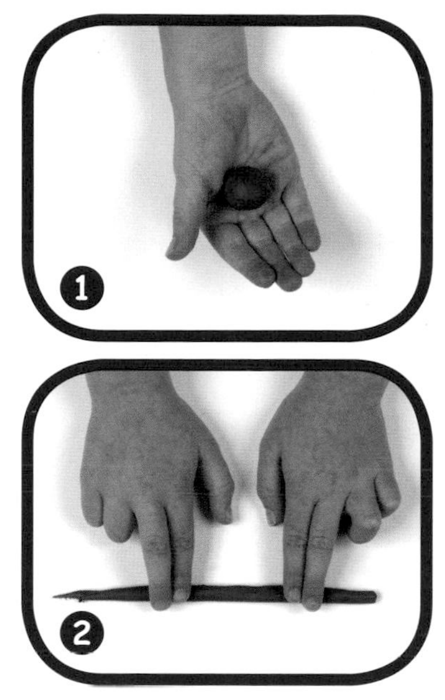

1. Create a ball shape following the Ball instructions.

2. Create a rope shape following the Rope instructions.

3. Lay the rope on the table. If you are concerned about the thickness, lay a craft stick on either side of the rope to measure.

4. Flatten the rope with a small rolling pin. Take care to press evenly with the rolling pin and roll from the center of the rope to one end. Pick up the pin, go back to the center, and roll to the other end. Always begin in the center and roll outward, as this will help keep the strips an even thickness as well as prevent them from sticking to the rolling pin.

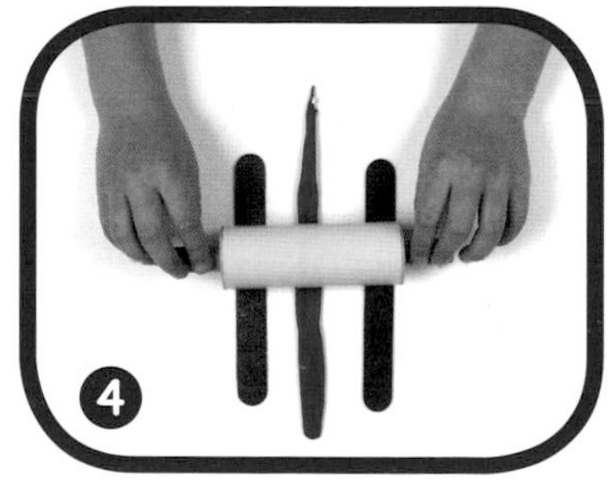

Cube:

1. Create a ball shape following the Ball instructions.

2. Take the ball and place it on a flat surface, then press down on the top of the ball to flatten it. Turn the ball over and repeat, until all six sides are flat. You can even the sides and smooth the corners with a flat object, such as a kitchen knife.

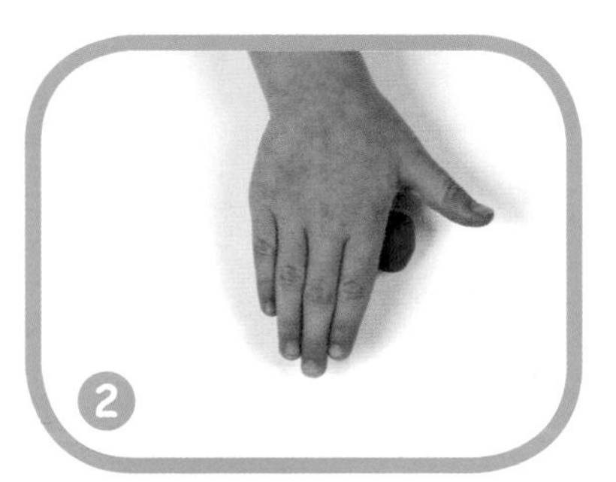

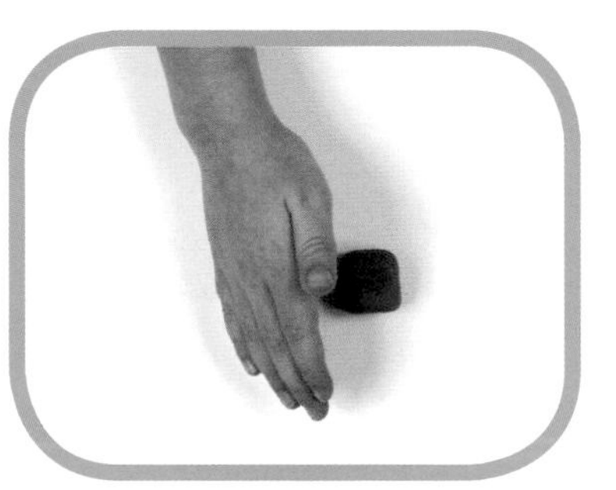

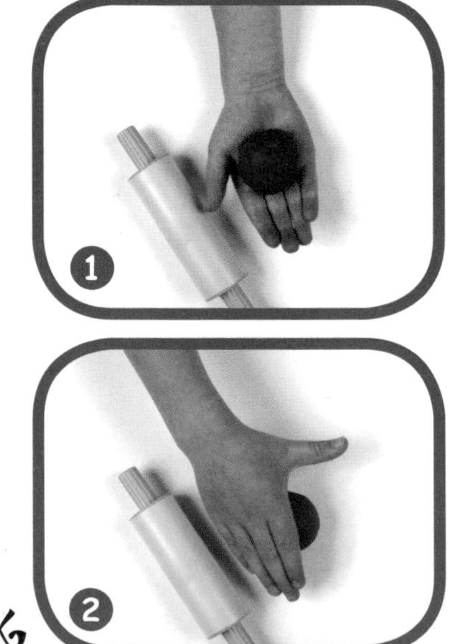

Slabs (square or round):

1. Create a large ball shape following the Ball instructions.

2. Lay the large ball on the table and flatten it slightly with the palm of your hand.

3. Flatten the ball with a small rolling pin following Step 4 under Strips.

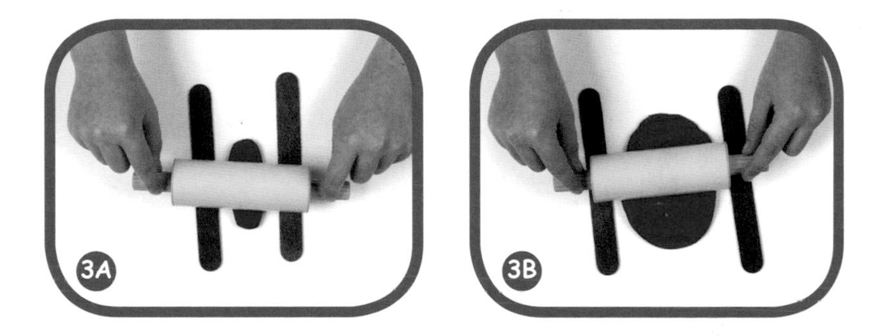

4. To make a square or round slab, cut out a square with a cookie cutter, a pattern, or use a ruler and a knife.

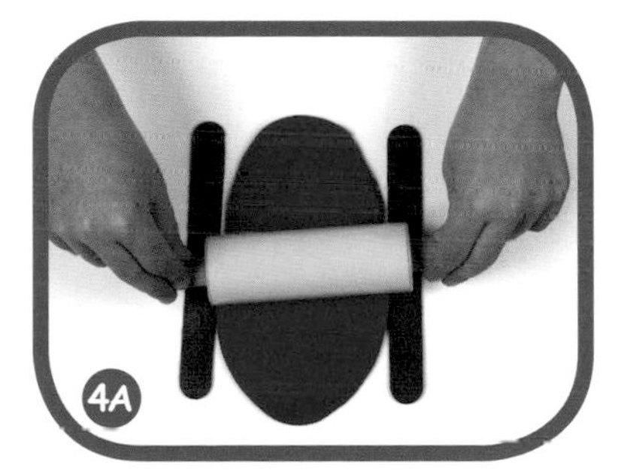

Small Circles:

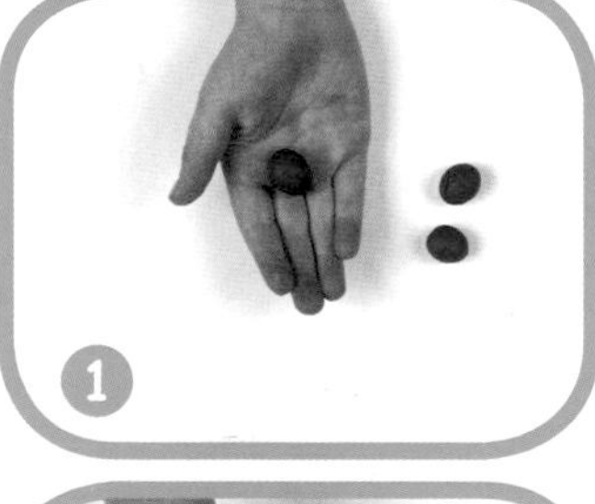

1. Create a small ball shape following the Ball instructions.

2. Place the ball on a flat surface and flatten with your thumb until it is the desired shape and thickness.

Making Simple Clay Canes:

A cane is a log made from polymer clay. It is created so that you have the same design running through the entire log. Once finished, you cut slices from the log in order to have repeats of the same image. The longer you make your cane, the more slices you will have. Canes can be made in any shape—circles, triangles, squares, stars, hearts, or anything else you wish.

General Cane Tips:

- Use the same type and brand of clay in your cane. Baking times and consistencies vary with manufacturers.
- If you are making a project to keep, allow the cane to sit overnight after creating it and before cutting it. The cane becomes warm and squishy after working with it, so the pieces may be distorted when cut. A shorter way is to put the finished cane in the refrigerator for 30 minutes.
- Your cane should be even from one end to the other before you begin cutting but if it isn't, don't worry. The design you have created may be more to your liking than one that is perfect!
- Store unused canes in airtight containers when not in use. If you put the canes into plastic bags for storage the canes may be squished during storage, distorting your designs.

Clay Dough Recipes

Basic Clay Dough

1 cup all-purpose flour

1 cup water

cup (125 mL) salt

1 teaspoon vegetable oil

teaspoon (2 mL) cream of tartar

Food coloring

1. Mix flour, water, salt, oil, and cream of tartar in a saucepan.
2. Cook over medium heat, mixing the entire time, until mixture holds together.
3. Let clay cool.
4. Knead on a floured surface.
5. Divide dough into smaller balls and add a different color of food coloring to each ball.
6. Knead color into dough.
7. Store each color in a separate airtight container.

Variation:

For intense colors use cake-decorating paste in place of food coloring.

Hint: Dough may be used over and over again and can be stored in the refrigerator for weeks.

Easy No-Cook Dough

This is the best dough to use with very young children who want to do everything themselves!

1 cup all-purpose flour
cup (90 mL) salt
cup (90 mL) hot water
Food coloring

1. Have child combine flour and salt in bowl.
2. Have adult pour in the hot water.
3. Child should stir mixture well.
4. Knead on lightly floured surface for at least 5 minutes.
5. Add a few drops of food coloring and continue to knead.
6. Store dough in airtight containers until needed.
7. Refrigerate up to 1 week

Variation:

For intense colors use cake decorating paste in place of food coloring.

Square Photo Holder

What You Need:

- 4 colors modeling clay
- Wire photo holder (can be purchased at your local craft or hobby store or you can make one by bending wire the shape you want)

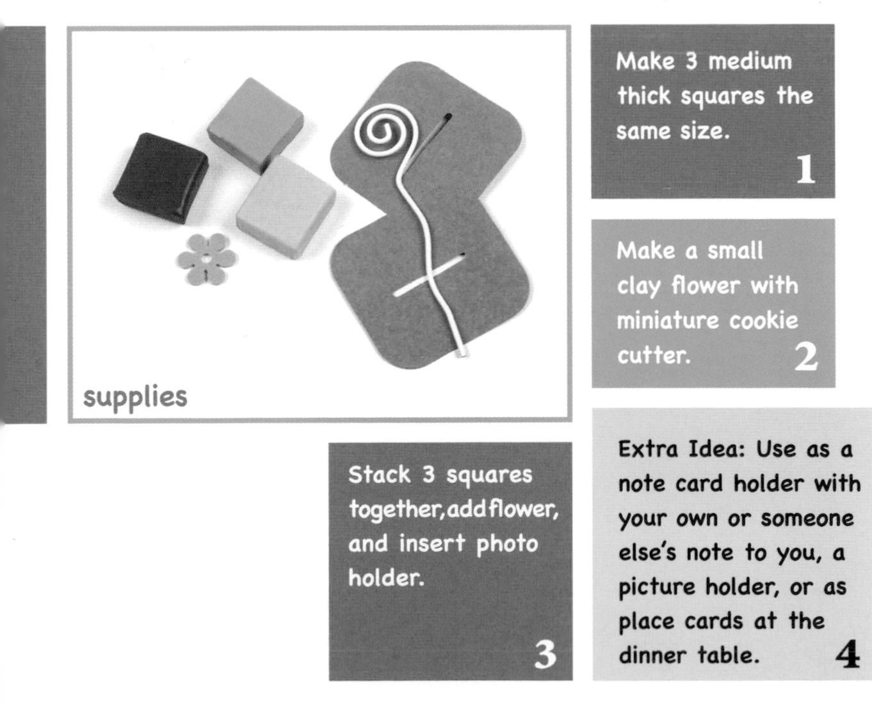

Make 3 medium thick squares the same size. **1**

Make a small clay flower with miniature cookie cutter. **2**

Stack 3 squares together, add flower, and insert photo holder. **3**

Extra Idea: Use as a note card holder with your own or someone else's note to you, a picture holder, or as place cards at the dinner table. **4**

Sailboat

What You Need:

- 4 colors modeling clay

Make a Ball and shape into a boat. 1

Make a Ball and shape into a triangle to make the sails - cut down middle. 2

Roll a Snake. Place under the bottom of the boat, bring up through triangle, and attach flag at the top as shown. 3

Airplane

What You Need:

- White modeling clay
- 4 additional colors of modeling clay

Make Slabs from each of the 4 colors modeling clay. Cut airplane shape from one slab. Cut wing shapes from one slab. 1

Cut propeller shape from one slab. Cut stars, small triangles, and circle from one slab. 2

Cut window from white slab. Layer shapes in this order: plane body, wings, stars, triangles, circle, window, propeller. 3

Lizard

What You Need:

- Green, black, orange modeling clay
- Wiggle eyes

1. Make Snake from orange clay, flatten into lizard body, and round one end as head.
2. Make 4 small Snakes, flatten, and place slightly under lizard body.
3. Make 12 small Balls. Place 3 on each leg, then flatten on top of each other to make lizard feet.
4. Make small green Snakes and decorate lizard tail.
5. Make small black Balls and decorate lizard body. Add wiggle eyes.

Ladybug

What You Need:

- Black, green, pink modeling clay
- Wiggle eyes

1. Make 2 Ovals from green clay and 1 Oval from black clay. Flatten all ovals between your hands so they are not so thick.
2. Put down black oval, place green ovals on top for wings. Make tiny pink Balls and decorate wings. Add wiggle eyes.

Chicken

What You Need:

- Black, orange, yellow modeling clay
- Extra-fine, black permanent marker
- Variety of clay colors for embellishments
- Feathers

Make a Slab from yellow clay. Cut into 1 large and 1 medium size circles. **1**

Wet top of large circle and place medium circle on top. Make a long, very skinny Snake from black clay. **2**

Take 3 pieces from the snake and make one leg, put the end up under the large circle and lightly press. **3**

Repeat with other leg. Make flower and head band for the chicken's hat and put on top of head. **4**

Make a triangle from orange clay for the beak and mark eyes with marker. Stick feathers into the clay around the top half of the body. **5**

Light Garland

What You Need:

- Black, green, red, white modeling clay
- Black string

Marble white and green clay together following Marbling directions on page 22. **1**

Repeat with white and red clay. Make marbled clay as well as red, green, white, and black clay into Slabs. **2**

Cut small circles from each of the slabs. Cut black circles in half. Squish black half circles onto colored circles. Lay on top of black string. **3**

Snowman

What You Need:

- Black, orange, red, white modeling clay

Make 1 Slab from both white and black clay. Cut 3 circles the same size from white clay. **1**

Cut a rectangle, a narrow strip, and 4 little squares from black clay. Layer circles to make a snowman. **2**

Add hat and circles. Make 2 Balls for eyes and a little pointed orange nose. Add tiny red Snake to hat to look like a ribbon. **3**

Beads

Beads made from Polymer Clay can be made using any of the techniques talked about in this book. You can marble the clay, twist snakes together, roll it into balls, make squares or triangles, cut shapes with tiny cookie cutters, and you can layer the clay to make dimensional objects. You can even paint the clay or glue glitter onto it when your projects are finished baking. The only thing you must remember to do is to punch a hole somewhere in the bead so that you can string it.

Use your imagination and make enough beads for everyone you know!

Flip-flop Bracelet

What You Need:

- A variety of colors of Polymer Clay
- Black elastic
- Small eyelets
- Toothpick

Make Balls from a variety of colors of clay. Flatten on 2 sides. Make holes through each ball with toothpick. **1**

Make flip-flops (page 38). Screw eyelets into top of flip-flops. Remove eyelets. **2**

Bake. Glue glitter to flip-flops. Re-insert eyelets, securing with glue. String onto elastic. **3**

Tips & Techniques for Fabulous Fun

Illustrated by Raffaella, Jessica, and Devin Dowling
Photography by F. William Lagaret
Text by Jessica Dowling

Painting on Rocks: Tips & Techniques for Fabulous Fun
Illustrated by Raffaella, Jessica, and Devin Dowling
Photography by F. William Lagaret
Text by Jessica Dowling

Mud Puddle Books, Inc.
54 W. 21st Street
Suite 601
New York, NY 10010
info@mudpuddlebooks.com

ISBN: 1-59412-167-2

Designed by Elsas Design

Printed and bound in China

Why Paint Rocks?

Rock painting is an easy and inexpensive way to create your own art! Painting rocks allows you to use your creativity in ways different than when you paint on paper or canvas. By studying the shape of the rock you can imagine all sorts of things that the rock could become.

What can I do with painted rocks?

Painted rocks make unique and expressive indoor or outdoor decorations. Put them on your mantle, your nightstand, or even use larger ones for bookends. They are great patio decorations, and a few tucked in a flowerpot always look pretty. Don't forget: painted rocks make wonderful gifts, too!

I don't know how to paint!

Rock painting is the perfect medium for beginners. If you mess up, just prime the rock over again and start out fresh. In addition, since the shape of the rock often suggests a form, it is easier for the beginning artist to pick a subject. Painting rocks is great for advanced artists, too! Challenge yourself and see how detailed your rocks can become. When someone mistakenly bites into a rock you've painted to look like a cookie, you're an expert!

What do I paint on a rock?

Anything! Paint your favorite animal or flower, or create a rock with a sports theme. Paint a letter on each of several rocks, and spell out your name or that of a friend. Paint vegetables or fruits on rocks to decorate a kitchen, or different sea creatures to decorate a bathroom. An apple-painted rock given to a teacher will last much longer than the real thing! The possibilities of what to paint are absolutely endless. Use your imagination!

Where can I find rocks?

Most arts and crafts stores sell smooth polished river stones. These have mostly round or oblong shapes; so if you want to find more unique rocks, get outside! Many rocks of varying shapes, sizes and textures can be found at the beach, or near rivers and lakes. If you live in a city, you can try looking for rocks in a park. Always make sure to have an adult with you when you go out looking for rocks.

Priming

Because rocks are often dark or bumpy, it is important to prime them before you paint your design. This prepares the rock to be painted on. To prime a rock, simply cover it with a thick coat of white paint and allow it to dry completely. It's okay if the rock's color still shows through; it will get covered up when you paint your design.

Materials

Acrylic Paint. A good basic set of paints would consist of white, black, red, blue, and yellow. You can mix most other colors you might want to use from these. You may, however, wish to invest in some extra paints since colors such as magenta and brown may be difficult to mix on your own. You'll find two-ounce bottles of acrylic craft paint are fairly inexpensive. They work great and cost much less than fine arts acrylics.

Acrylic brushes in several sizes. Consider starting out with a size 6 filbert, a size 4 round, and a size 0 round (for fine details). Try out different brush sizes as you determine your artistic needs.

Clear acrylic glaze to protect rocks that are displayed outside or to give your indoor rocks a brilliant sheen. This glaze comes in aerosol cans or in liquid form to be painted on. Use the liquid form for painting rocks because it adheres better, and you can apply it indoors. A small bottle (around 120 ml) should last a long time.

Toothpicks. These are great for painting tiny details or dots.

A cup of water to clean brushes.

Paper towels for surface cleanup.

Newspaper to lay on top of your work area and protect surfaces.

A pencil to sketch out your design on the rock. A soft pencil works best, as it will show up on the rock better. Instead of a standard #2 pencil, pick up a soft 6B pencil at an art supply store.

Scrap paper to jot down ideas. Always keep some paper with you in case a great idea for a painted rock strikes you when you are on the go!

Pet Rocks

Holiday Rocks

Sporty Rocks

Nature Rocks

Rock Pirates

Rock Designs

MAKING FRIENDSHIP BRACELETS

By Kaylee Conner

Mud Puddle Books
NEW YORK

Making Friendship Bracelets
by Kaylee Conner

Mud Puddle Books, Inc.
54 W. 21st Street Suite 601
New York, NY 10010

ISBN: 978-1-59412-149-2

Printed in China

INTRODUCTION

What exactly is a friend? Webster's dictionary defines friend "as someone who is not an enemy." To us, friends can be classmates, roommates, companions, confidantes, soul mates, allies, collaborators, teammates, peers, or supporters. A friend is a person that helps you, encourages you, questions you when she is in doubt, has fun with you, works with you, stands by you when you need her, and finally, needs you as much as you need her. A friend can be a casual friend, a good friend, a close friend, or your very best friend.

A friend is a person you want to do something nice for, whether it's a special occasion like their birthday, or just because it's Tuesday and you feel like it. A friend is a person that you want to thank in a "you're special to me" sort of handmade way.

That is why making friendship bracelets—for a friend or with a friend—is so much more meaningful than something store-bought. It's a special gift that you made with her in mind, something just for her. Remember, if it is made by hand, it comes from the heart.

Friendship bracelets are easy, fun, and inexpensive. You can make one or one hundred! Making unique bracelets for any occasion is simple—make them casual or dressy; beaded or plain; or from thread, ribbons, or strips of fabric. Your imagination is all you need to be a designer extraordinaire of friendship bracelets.

SUPPLIES

THREAD OR FLOSS:

Traditional six-strand embroidery thread, usually called embroidery floss, is most often used to make friendship bracelets.

SPECIALTY FIBERS:

Pearl cotton, knitting yarns, thin ribbons, soft silk-like fabrics, and specialty threads of any type can be used to make friendship bracelets.

TIPS

Make certain that the colors of the thread you are using will not bleed when wet. If you spend the time to make someone a friendship bracelet, you do not want it to get ruined.

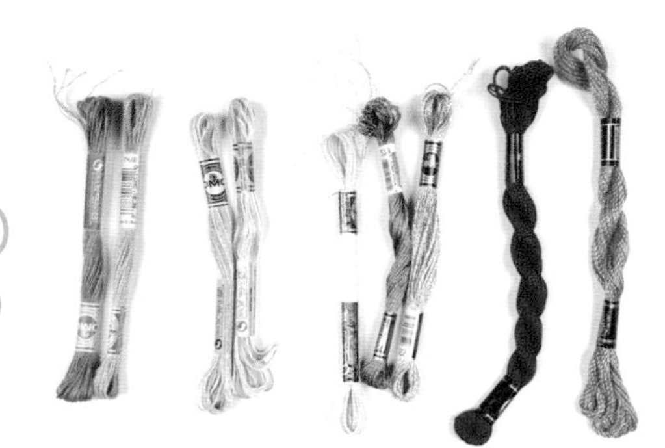

Designer Secret:
The colors and textures of specialty fibers add a "designer touch" to even a simple project. Use them by themselves, or mix-and-match to make a variety of bracelets.

CLIPBOARD:

This book will refer to using a knotting board (see page 94), but you may prefer to use a clipboard rather than cardboard and pins to hold your bracelet while you are making it. This will secure the bracelet at the top, but you will be unable to pin the knots in place as you work.

KNOTTING BOARD:

We recommend creating a knotting board by using a thick piece of cardboard—such as the side of a box—to use as a work surface for creating your friendship bracelets. The board should be firm, yet allow you to easily insert and remove pins. Use large hatpins to secure your knots in place.

TIPS

By marking the end length of your bracelet on the knotting board or clipboard, you will know at a glance just how long the bracelet needs to be.

BEADS:

Beads of any type and size can be used to embellish your friendship bracelets. You will want to make certain that the thread or fiber you are using will fit through the hole of the bead. If you have difficulty getting the thread through the bead hole, you can use a beading wire loop (see page 95) to help you. If the bead hole is just too small, try adding a length of thin, 24-gauge wire to your threads. The beads will easily slip onto the wire.

BEADING WIRE LOOP:

This loop is optional, but can make it easier to add beads to your bracelet. Simply take a thin piece of 24-gauge wire, bend, and wrap as show in diagram.

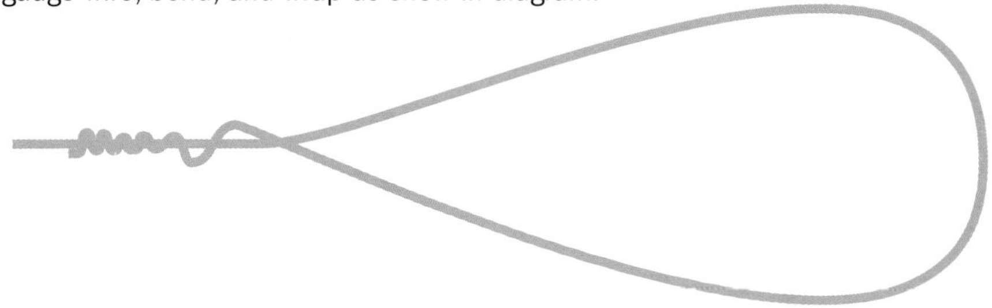

EMBELLISHMENTS:

Almost anything can be used to adorn friendship bracelets. Charms for jewelry-making, small craft items such as miniature Christmas garlands, or a multitude of scrapbooking embellishments can be added. Walk up and down the aisles of your favorite fabric or craft store and see all of the wonderful things that can be used.

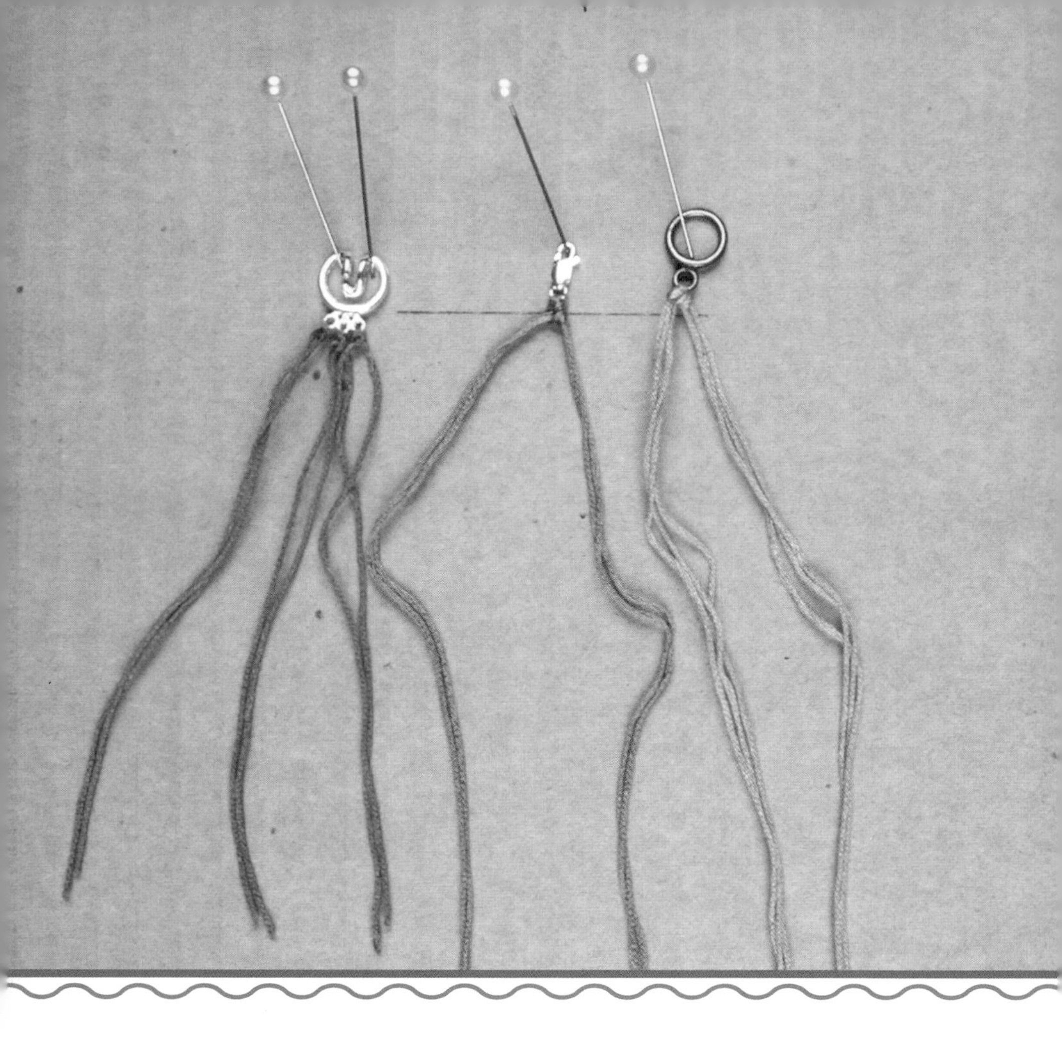

JEWELRY CLOSURES:

Jewelry closures are optional; however, they make removing your friendship bracelet a snap! See Ending Your Bracelet on page 101.

MISCELLANEOUS TOOLS AND MATERIALS:

24-Gauge Beading Wire
Fabric Glue
Ruler
Scissors

BASIC KNOTS

There are 3 basic knots used to make friendship bracelets in this book. They are easy to master and easy to remember, but you may want to practice a little before beginning to make your first friendship bracelet. A little practice now will save a considerable amount of frustration, time, and materials.

OVERHAND KNOTS

This knot can be created with as few as 2 threads, but you can use as many threads as you like.

Right Overhand Knot

Step 1

Measure at least 2 threads to be 4 times the length of the finished bracelet. (Double the length if you will be folding the threads in half before you start knotting.)

Tightly hold the left-hand thread and knot the remaining thread around it.

Step 2

Pull thread to the right until tight.

Step 3

Repeat

Step 4

Finished complete knot

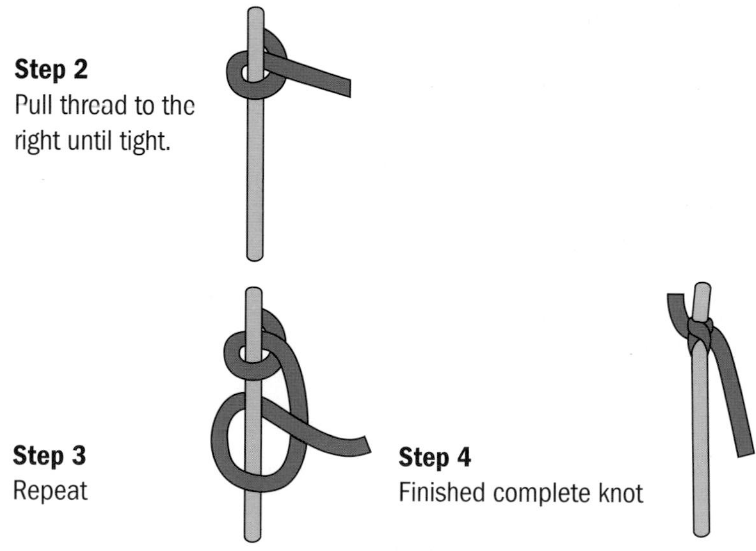

Reminder: *A complete overhand knot is always tied twice.*

Left Overhand Knot

Step 1

Measure at least 2 threads to be 4 times the length of the finished bracelet. (Double the length if you will be folding the threads in half before you start knotting.)

Tightly hold the right-hand thread and knot the remaining thread around it.

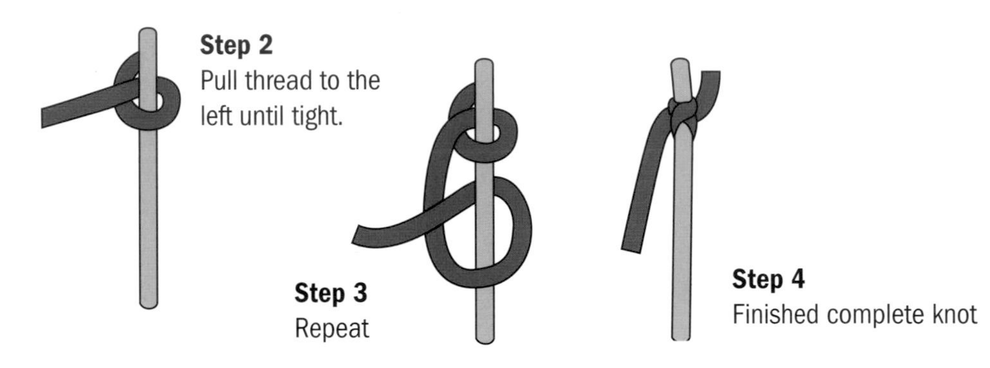

Step 2
Pull thread to the left until tight.

Step 3
Repeat

Step 4
Finished complete knot

Notes:

1. *In this book the overhand knot is sometimes completed as a right overhand knot and sometimes as a left overhand knot, but either way it is the same knot.*
2. *The overhand knot can be made with as many threads as you want.*

Reminder: *A complete overhand knot is always tied twice.*

SQUARE KNOT

Step 1
Measure each of 4 strands to be 4 times the desired length of the finished bracelet. Knot the strands together at one end, and pin the knot to the knotting board. Separate the strands.

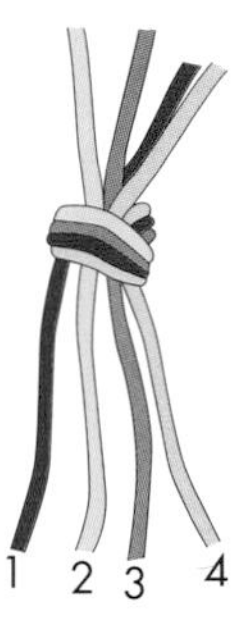

Step 2
Move thread #4 from the far right and cross it over the center threads (#2 and #3) and under thread #1.

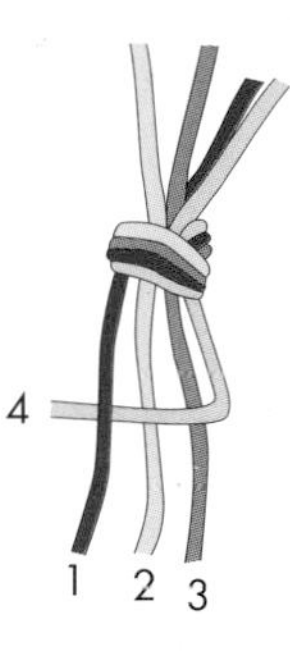

Step 3
Move thread #1 over thread #4 and under threads #2 and #3.

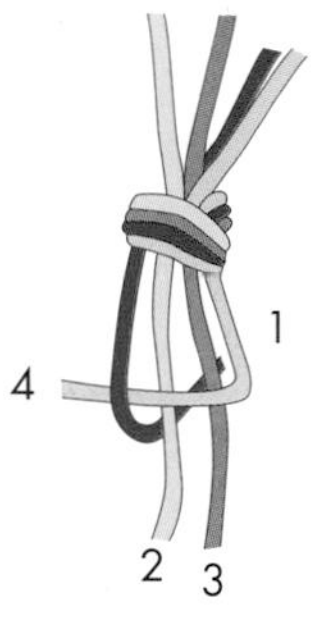

Step 4
Bring thread #1 from behind through the loop in thread #4 (far right).

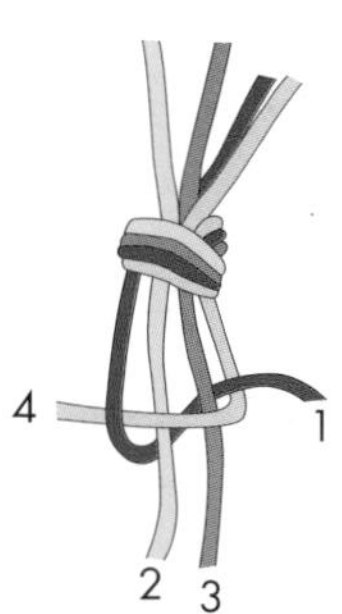

Step 5
Pull on threads #1 and #4 to create the first half of the square knot.

Step 6
Move thread #4 from the left and cross it over the center strands (#2 and #3) and under thread #1.

Step 7
Bring thread #1 under threads #2 and #3 and through the loop on the far left.

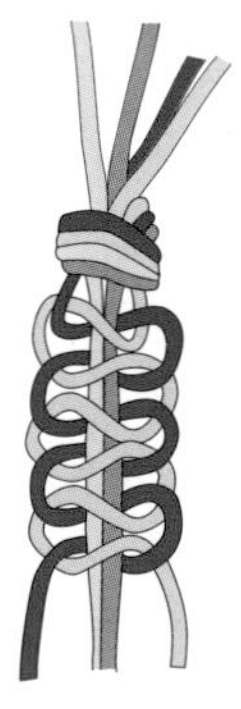

Step 8
Pull on threads #1 and #4 to finish the square knot.

ENDING YOUR BRACELET

Each of the projects in this book tells how to end the bracelet as it is pictured in the example. However, the following endings can be used with any of the bracelets you learn to make, so feel free to make any substitutions.

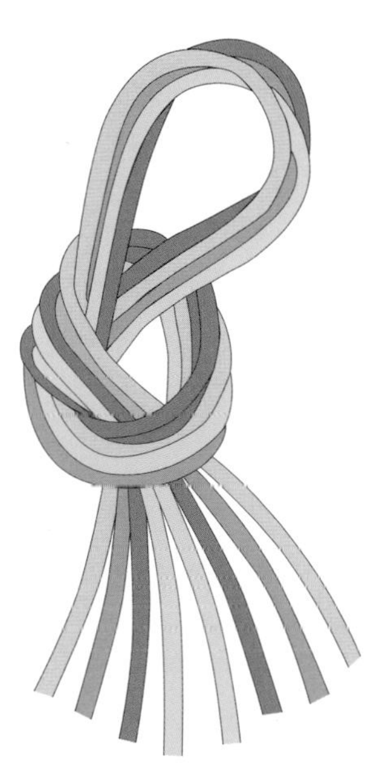

POSSIBILITY 1: LOOPED-END BRACELET

Folding the threads in half when starting the bracelet will create a loop at one end that can be used for tying bracelet ends together.

To Wear:
Wrap the finished bracelet around your wrist. Divide the threads at the loose end, and slip one half the threads through the loop. Tie to the other half of the threads, securing in a double knot so that the bracelet does not come untied.

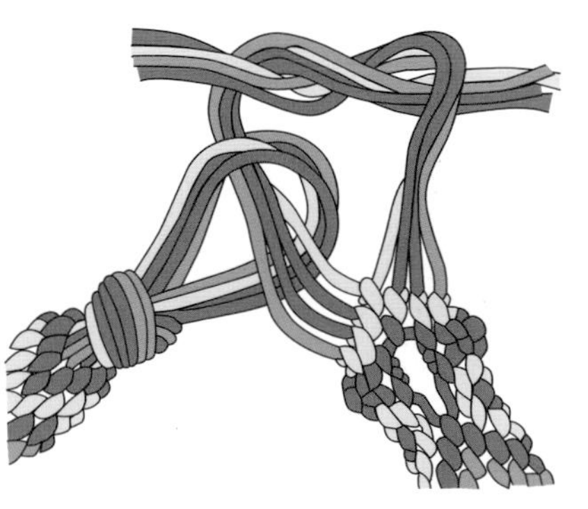

POSSIBILITY 2: LOOSE-ENDS BRACELET

This bracelet is made by using single strands of thread that are not folded in half and looped.

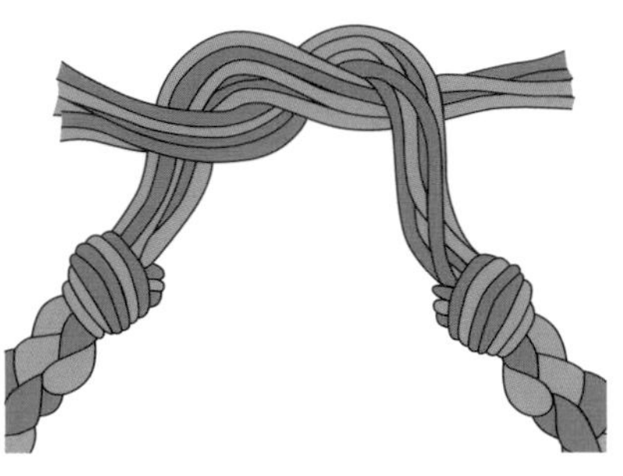

To Wear:
Wrap the finished bracelet around your wrist. Tie ends together in a double knot, cutting longer ends to desired length.

TIPS

Fastening your bracelets with Possibility 1 or Possibility 2 is best for those that will be worn until you tire of them. Tying and untying the threads will eventually fray them, making it difficult to tie a secure knot.

POSSIBILITY 3: JEWELRY CLOSURE BRACELET

These bracelets have jewelry closures at both ends just like traditional jewelry, making it possible to remove the bracelet as often as desired.

The closures are easiest to attach when the bracelet is made from 3 or 4 strands of embroidery floss. After tying the closures to the bracelet ends, you may need to place a small amount of fabric glue over the knots to keep them secure.

To Wear:
Attach this bracelet to your wrist just as you would attach any piece of traditional jewelry.

The projects found in this book employ fun and easy techniques. Just follow the step-by-step instructions to create fabulous designs for you and your friends.

BASIC WRAPPED BRACELET

This easy bracelet requires a flexible core thread to wrap the threads of the bracelet around. Mix up the size of your bracelets by using a thin or thick core—and wear them singly or all together.

MATERIALS:

Core thread, thin
Embroidery floss, 1 color

STEP 1

Cut core thread to desired length of finished bracelet plus a little for finishing. Cut 2 strands of embroidery floss to 4 times the length of the core thread, tie both strands of floss to the core. Be sure to leave a long enough tail to tie your bracelet onto your wrist.

STEP 2

Pin the core thread to the knotting board. Tightly wrap both strands of floss around the core thread to the end and tie in a knot.

STEP 3

Wrap finished bracelet around wrist and tie floss ends together in a double knot. If ends are too long, trim to desired length.

WRAPPED BRACELET WITH ALTERNATING COLORS

Want to add a little variety to your wrapped bracelets? This simple bracelet alternates colors to let you and your friends show off your school colors, your club colors, or just your favorite colors.

MATERIALS:

Core thread, thin
Embroidery floss, 2 colors

STEP 1

Cut core thread to desired length of finished bracelet plus a little for finishing. Cut 2 strands of each color embroidery floss to 4 times the length of the core thread, tie all strands of floss to the core. Be sure to leave a long enough tail to tie your bracelet onto your wrist.

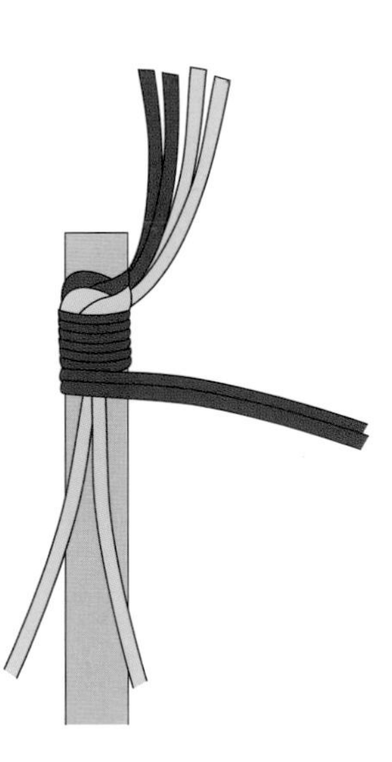

STEP 2

Pin the core thread to the knotting board. Tightly wrap the 2 strands of the first color of floss around the core and the second color of floss until you have the desired amount of color.

STEP 3

Pick up the strands of the second color floss and tightly wrap around both the core thread and the first color of floss until you have the desired amount of color.

Repeat Steps 2 and 3, alternating colors as desired until you reach the end of the core thread. Knot tightly at the end of the core thread.

STEP 5

Wrap finished bracelet around wrist and tie floss ends together in a double knot. If ends are too long, trim to desired length.

WRAPPED BRACELET WITH TWISTED THREAD

MATERIALS:

Thin cord, 1 color
Core thread, thick
Embroidery floss, 1 color

STEP 1

Cut core thread to desired length of finished bracelet plus a little for finishing. Cut 2 strands of embroidery floss and 2 strands of thin cord to 4 times the length of the core thread, tie both strands of floss to the core. Be sure to leave a long enough tail to tie your bracelet onto your wrist.

STEP 2

Tie thin cord to the core thread directly beneath the floss.

STEP 3

Pin the core thread to the Knotting Board. Wrap the 2 embroidery floss strands around the core thread and thin cords for about ½" (1.3 cm).

STEP 4

Pull the thin cords up and move them out of the way. Continue wrapping core thread with embroidery floss to the end. Knot tightly at the end of the core threads.

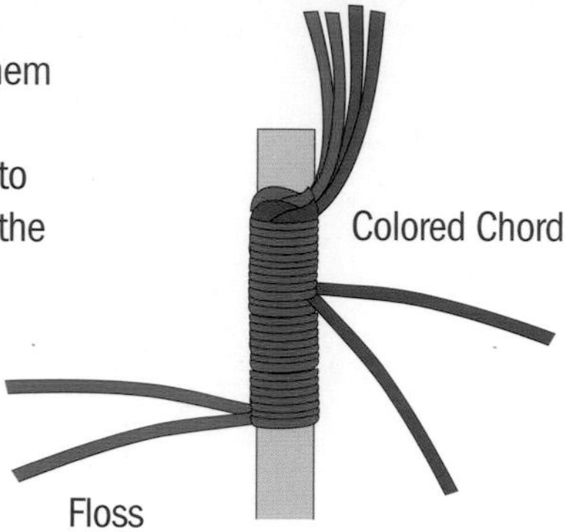

Colored Chord

Floss

STEP 5

Twist thin cord strands together and wrap the thin cords around the floss-wrapped core. When the cord reaches the end of the solid color floss place thin cords next to core thread and wrap with floss. Tie floss and thin cords into a tight knot.

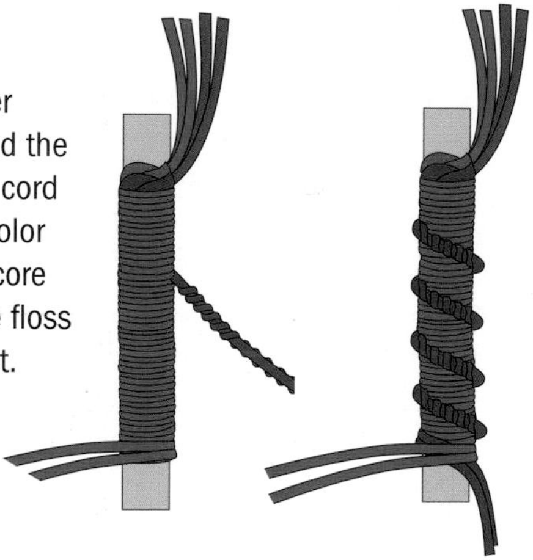

STEP 6

Wrap finished bracelet around wrist and tie floss ends together in a double knot. If ends are too long, trim to desired length.

Designer Secret:
For this variation string thin cord with beads, do not twist, wrap around wrapped core.

HAPPY BIRTHDAY

1-2-3 BRACELET

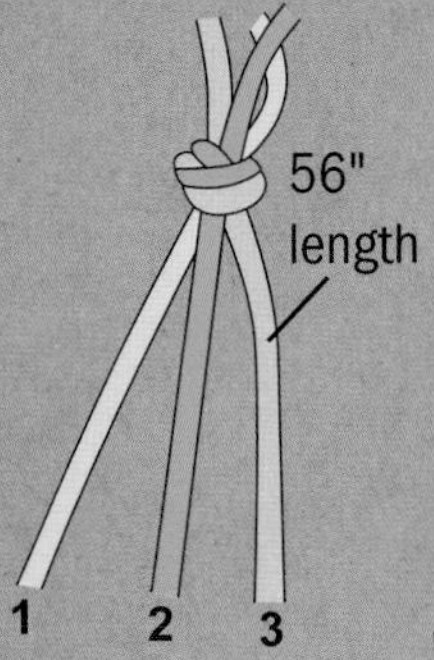

56"
length

1 2 3

STEP 1

Cut a length of all 3 colors of floss 3 times the desired length of the finished bracelet. Tie all 3 lengths together and pin knot to knotting board, then separate threads as shown in diagram.

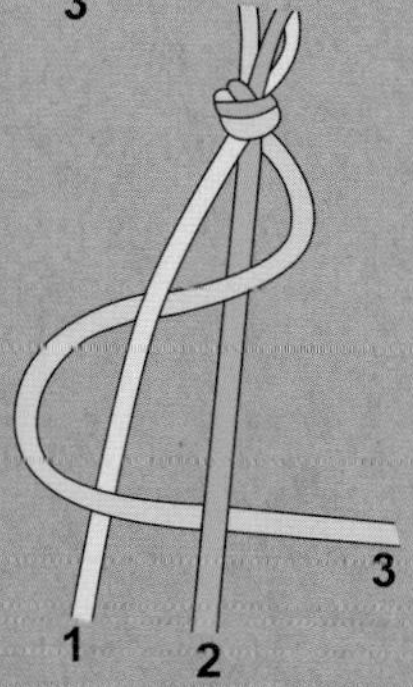

3

1 2

STEP 2

Weave the #3 thread over the #2 thread and under the # 1 thread, then over the #1 and under the #2 thread. Be careful to hold the threads straight and tight while you weave.

3

1 2

STEP 3

Hold the #1 and #2 threads with one hand and pull the #3 thread so that the weaving slides up the bracelet toward the top knot. Continue weaving for desired length.

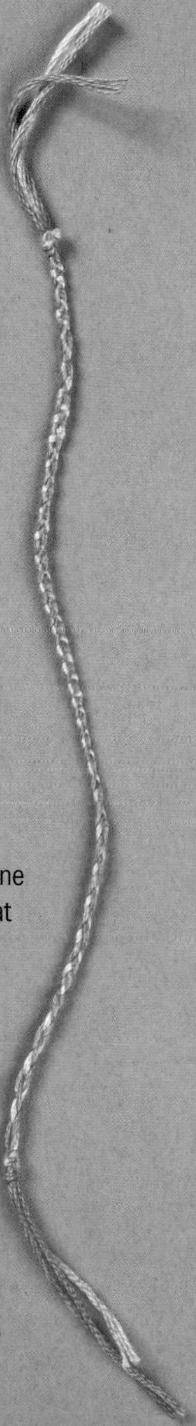

MATERIALS:

Beads
Embroidery floss, 3 colors

STEP 4

Tie a knot at the end of the bracelet. Wrap finished bracelet around your wrist and tie thread ends together in a double knot. If ends are too long, trim to desired length.

Designer Secret:
For this bracelet create several woven strands plus 1 strand of beads strung on 24-gauge wire. At end of each strand secure a crimp bead and attach to jump ring and jewelry clasp. An easy alternative is to tie all strands and wire together in a knot at both ends of the bracelet and wrap around wrist.

Designer Secret:
Simply string typewriter beads over woven threads. Typewriter beads can be found in the scrapbooking section of your local craft store.